Mindful Survival

by

Holbrook Breckenridge

RoseDog❈Books
PITTSBURGH, PENNSYLVANIA 15238

RoseDog Books
585 Alpha Drive
Suite 103
Pittsburgh, PA 15238
Visit our website at *www.rosedogbookstore.com*

ISBN: 978-1-6442-6517-8
eISBN: 978-1-6442-6540-6

Dedication

This book has been dedicated in loving memory to my fallen mother, Kalena. Always my rock, paper, and scissors. She was the first to tell me to cut it out. The one to endure the day-in-and-day-out grind to ensure that I had a sense of self and always first to step up to sacrifice so much more than a monetary value. Truly, my lost world.

Best regards to the vast number of individuals that made this book possible. The considerations and contributions are too great for anyone to repay upon looking at the experience that I have been blessed to receive in the context of overwhelming endearment. My only hope is for all to remain youthful within the aspect of enjoying one's life. At my core I feel as though we are all surviving under the same sky, and be it as it may, regarding any and all differences, that is nonetheless common ground. Respectively yours....

Introduction

People do many different things at various times for many different reasons. Within the bounds of this book, you will see one man's perception of the road he traveled through years of hard work and deliberation from within and along the road to self-liberation From fear to fantasy, from joy to pain, and from illness to rehabilitation, these extremes are all within the context of my life in this autobiography.

This book will show my efforts to develop a sense of self in a family and environmental context by which facts have both supported and hindered my efforts to survive in a world that takes no prisoners. Where fear became a reality, fantasy an escape, joy embraced elation, and pain became surreal.

Contents

Chapter 1

A Glazed Look at a World of Fear

In this book, I will attempt to walk you through my world as it was compiled of insecurities and fears, molestation, drug abuse, childhood pregnancy, mental illness, and its rehabilitation. I will discuss where I was then, who I was then, and who I survived to be today.

In retrospect, I can only delve into parts of my past through a hazed memory or gaze if you will. It is only through a hazed memory that I am able to reflect back on periods of time within my life to bring to the surface what each period meant for me. Each period of time is a frame that stands still.

My mother's very first recollection of how much my sister did not want me in her life took place the day she brought me home, an infant wrapped in a blanket. She told me that while she was changing my diaper I began to scream. It was not because of a diaper pin stick but because of my two-year-old sister Jennifer biting my feet. This would prove to be prevalent treatment from her throughout my years to follow.

When I was two years old, my parents divorced. My father left my mother for another woman. My mother's boyfriends' and my school instructors would soon become my only male role models throughout my childhood. Until I was thirteen my older sister was my distant playmate who really did not want to be bothered with a younger brother. Because she was older than me, she played the role of the boss. Jennifer and I would fight over trivial things such as the remote control for the television as well as toys and games. She would make it very clear that her friends were her friends and my friends were just children. It was obvious to me that she simply did not want me around her. When my mother and father divorced, my father remarried soon afterwards and my new stepmother Florance had a daughter Diane. Diane seemed nice but since she did not live with us I did not have much contact with her. I now found myself with a half-sister in my life. Life seemed to tug along. It was tough being the only male growing up with two females. My sister and mother fought like cats and dogs. I felt like I should be able to stop the squabbling and make things right between them. This self-inflicted pressure was too much for a mere child to take on. This pressure would culminate into a much bigger problem for me down the road when it became compounded with what was yet to come.

I'll jump forward to age thirteen. I was in junior high school. I was quite the class clown, a role I assumed to combat insecurities that set in due to my dysfunctional home life. I was also failing PE. My coach was a jerk. To my dismay my mother met him one day while dropping me off at school. She asked who he was with a bit of attraction in her voice. I cringed and told her he was a jerk. She stopped to talk to him and the next thing I knew they were engaged. I started behaving in his class in order to avoid getting in trouble at home. Before long our home was being rearranged for the convenience of Jack and his two daughters Simone and Lori. Simone was one year younger than me and Lori was one year older than me. Both were attractive, Simone with blonde hair and Lori with brown hair. Both were athletic and very popular in school. They both had more of an uptown air about them than that of the Westbank culture of New Orleans. They seemed nice to me but it was obvious that Lori did not care much for Jennifer.

As the wedding neared, big problems arose between my sister Jennifer and my mother based on incidents between Jennifer and Jack. One night Jennifer went to a party that relocated from a friend's house to a hotel room. When her ride got too drunk to drive her home she called my mom to come get her. The next day Jack told my mother that Jennifer should have called her the moment she found out the party was moved to a hotel room. When he tried to punish Jennifer she told him that he was not her dad so she did not have to take orders from him. The dissension between the two caused Jack to break off his engagement to my mother. He did not want to bring his two daughters into the house with Jennifer. Jennifer and I were already in the process of moving her things from the upstairs bedroom to the downstairs bedroom so that Jack's daughters could move in. My mother presented Jennifer with a total change of plans. She told her she had to move out of the house so that she could marry Jack. I could only imagine how stunned and hurt Jennifer must have felt our mother choosing a man over her. As mean as Jennifer had been to me I felt so bad for her. The foundation of our single parent household cracked. Jennifer did not have much of a choice so she agreed to leave home and live with friends so my mother could get remarried. It was a difficult situation for my sister. She felt nothing but contempt and betrayal from my mother and I felt that I could be thrown out of my house as well if I did not get along with my mothers' fiancé and his two daughters.

Being the only boy in my home brought on many tasks that differed from a nuclear family. I found that much of how I reacted to certain situations was due to my upbringing. My mother and several of her friends told me as I was growing up that because my father was absent I would have to take on the new role of being the man of the house. This role meant for me taking care of my mother and Jennifer. This task proved difficult. My mother constantly focused on the bleak and dark side of life. Because being a single parent, there were always responsibilities to be shared. She often appeared to be desperately trying to survive the adversities that life dealt her. Consequently Jennifer and I felt that we had to be adults to help carry some of the weight; we were only children taking on the roles of adults. On many occasions, Jennifer and I played the role of caregiver to my mother. My mother has always painted life in the grimmest light. Growing up, I remember her being consumed by the news as well as the obituaries in the daily newspaper. She was always talking about people dying, crime, and how difficult life was. Because of this, confusion and anxiety began at an early age for me. Fantasy became my only escape and fear became the norm.

In addition to these fears, I also suffered much insecurity because I was of a small build. I had been picked on much of my home life by Jennifer; and at school I found myself playing the role of a bully in order to combat the abuse I had at home. I encountered much discipline, however, from the teachers within the elementary school that I attended but I felt as though negative attention was better than no attention at all. I was confused and my temper only made things worse. I would exercise my "fight or flight" mechanism and often there were times that I chose to fight and found myself in several fistfights. A lot of bottled up frustration was surfacing much of which was caused within my dysfunctional family. I learned to talk a good game and played the role of a class clown. I found that I was consistently protecting myself by engaging in childhood warfare, running like a scared rabbit or playing the role of a jokester to keep people at bay. A child from a healthy home life would not experience such strain full emotions.

Going backward, it was at only age five that my mother decided to put me in summer camp. My first year was day camp, then I upgraded to overnight camp for one month. By the age of seven I would be away at camp for a full six weeks during the summer. Eventually I was going from New Orleans to Tennessee every summer for two months for a total of five years. My mother was sending Jennifer and me off to summer camp every summer. Jennifer quit going at the age of thirteen because she wanted to stay home and hang out with her friends. I would continue to go alone until I completed the "Master's Program," which was the highest program that the camp had to offer. I achieved the "All American Camper" award at age fifteen. When I was eight years old, however, I was attending a different camp in Merry hill, Louisiana, when a strange encounter happened. This encounter would be one determining factor that would alter my thinking of my own sexuality for years to come. This incident happened one summer when I came in from the soccer field. It was time for dinner so I went back to the dormitory to change out of my sweaty clothes. As I was changing, a counselor persuaded me to allow him to perform fellatio on me. After this horrible incident I finally pushed him off. He threatened that if I told anyone what had just happened, he would find my family and me and kill us. I was petrified! I did, however, experience a twisted sense of control. On one hand I felt as though I was now the protector of myself and my family, and on the other, I was the determining factor of our fate. We could live or die based on whether or not I would keep this terrible secret. I was confused for a long time because of the sexual encounter as well as the threat. Because of the fact that I got an erection, I would question my sexuality for several years after. I thought that I had finally come to grips with this incident at age eleven. I decided to tell my mom. She was in complete denial. Psychiatric therapy would become a great tool to help me overcome this traumatic experience in the future. It took a long time to realize that it was not my fault and the erection was a natural physical response to stimulation. Because I had been molested and the perpetrator told me that he just wanted to see what it tasted like, as I grew up I often wondered what it was that he experienced. Because of the uncomfortable feelings that I had endured, I was compelled to do the right thing. I did not want to victimize anyone the way I had been. This is what I believe kept me from experimentation with anyone else. The memory is still vivid in my mind and it will always be part of my past.

During the same period of time; from the time I was eight years old until I was eleven, my mother would trust our next-door neighbor to watch Jennifer and me while she would go out at night. Our babysitter was about two years older than me. She would often have Jennifer and me sleep in the same bed with her. On many occasions she would sleep half naked and would entice me to kiss and fondle her while Jennifer was lying next to her. For me I could only hope that Jennifer was asleep, but I was never really sure. I was afraid of getting into trouble. I can remember two occasions where the babysitter tried to get me to seduce her. My penis was erect while her underwear was off. I did not do anything because of a story that I heard about the king that inserted a razor blade inside of his daughter's vagina for the purpose of cutting off any man's penis that tried to seduce her. I honestly believed that if I entered her body with my penis that it would be cut off. The truth of the matter was that I was too scared to go through with it. The babysitter once asked me when we came close to engaging in sex if I had sperm. I remember asking what that was and she said that it was yellow stuff that came out of my penis. I told her no only to recall later that I do urinate. That is an example of our immaturity at a very young and vulnerable age.

I recall another incident when I was nine years old. My fourth grade teacher was an ex-nun. She was extremely strict on her students. It was clear to me that she aspired to be so. She picked mostly on the boys of the class. There was a time when she stood me up in front of the class to have the entire class laugh at me because I had ugly shoes on. It was an uptown school and I felt like I was too poor to belong. I was very embarrassed in front of my peers. I felt extremely small in front of the class. I thought the only thing that cared about me was my dog. It became evident that I was in a lot of emotional pain and confusion. I was not the happy go lucky kid that I should have been.

My mother picked up on signs of my depression and readily put me in touch with a social worker. At this point a man had molested me at camp. Molested by the babysitter and degraded in front of my peers by a nun. I ended up failing the reading class so I went to a reading and math camp during that summer so I could pass to the fifth grade at a different school. The social worker did not do much with me. He mainly taught me how to play chess talked a little bit about my home life and finally discharged me from his services. That was the first of several encounters that I would have with psychotherapy throughout my life. The attention that I was given appeared to be positive. We talked for many months about my home life as well as about my dad. The social worker was a real inspiration. He made every session strictly on my terms and I was put at ease to do or talk about anything that I chose. He was not pushy and he related to me as a friend and not someone of authority. Up to this point the only authority figures who stood out in my life were my mother, my father and the camp counselor who molested me. It was after the molestation that I began to have a problem with authority figures. The fact that my social worker dealt with me on a level of friendship opposed to an authoritative view made my sessions successful. My mother also had my sister Jennifer see the social worker as well. It was his advice to have both of us go through therapy, including my mother. I do not know what the therapist did with Jennifer in her sessions. To this day Jennifer does not elaborate about the sessions. I believe the social worker brought her into sessions due to comments I made about our squabbling and dysfunctional family life. My mother sometimes sat in sessions with us but she never attended sessions for herself. I would find out later on down the line that the psychiatrist assigned to Jennifer and I would express deep concerns about our mother's need for psychotherapy.

I want to address another obsession of my mother and sisters behavior that added major pressure on me regarding my self-image. My mother and Jennifer were a major driving force in a quest for me to have a girlfriend. Growing up I would see them getting dressed in the morning before school as well as hear them talk at night. They imposed on me the idea that only successful, good looking and wealthy men are eligible to have girlfriends and wives. I can remember being in the fourth grade when one morning my hair would not comb a certain way. I became so frustrated that I broke the glass on my mother's' dresser with the brush. I was trying desperately to be good looking so that I could live up to their description of a successful guy. I grew up watching my mother and Jennifer make such a fuss over the way they looked that it rubbed off on me. It was as if not being good looking enough to get a girlfriend meant that you were some kind of failure. Needless to say, I was under a lot of social pressure for only being nine years old.

In the absence of a father in the house, I became clingy to my mother and to Jennifer. Jennifer and I would quite frequently bicker over trivial things. As we got older and into our teenage years more heated confrontations would erupt between her and my mother. I found myself more often than not trying to defend my mother as time went on, even though I loved them both. Jennifer was at times very overpowering and physical. I remember one incident when she was approximately sixteen years old. She punched my mother in the mouth and caused her crown to fall out. Jennifer wanted to go out and my mother was against it and that was when Jennifer decided to use physical force to overpower my mother. However, as we got older Jennifer and I became closer as brother and sister and my mother and I became closer as mother and son. If all three of us were together, on the other hand, it was a free for all and I was the umpire who was constantly trying to break up the fighting. Even when I tried to stay out of the arguments they would drag me back into them to determine who was right and who was wrong. I believe that if we had had better boundaries, mainly better guidelines as to what was and was not appropriate behavior, much of the squabbling would not have taken place. Better boundaries would have stopped us from getting entwined in each other's business to the point that if one of us was unhappy (or had a bad day,) then all of us were to be unhappy (or have a bad day). Better boundaries would have given us safer and more secure feelings about one another as well as define expectations and limits. This would have enabled us to have a clearer understanding to work from instead of a dysfunctional outlook on everything.

Chapter 2

Family History

A fantasizing childhood from a broken home's perception
The confusion of being a preteen

Fantasy became a way for me to escape. My fantasy brought to light creativity and a sense of humor. The creativity made me aspire to be somewhat different than mainstream society. I was constantly being a class clown in order to make people laugh. As I grew older and more skilled at making light of situations, peers would say that I was a jokester and should consider a life as a standup comic. I found humor to be a way of easing uncomfortable situations and used it for controlling situations and for diffusing fights. On the surface this would appear to be good, however much pain from within caused by dysfunctional relationships began to take its toll on me, as I grew older. I was the funny little clown laughing on the outside and crying on the inside. My life began to evolve around pleasing everyone at the expense of spreading myself too thin. This pressure began in my home with me being the only man who should be fixing things and making everything right for my mom and Jennifer. This pressure was progressing from me believing that I had to fix my family to me believing, as I got older, that I had to somehow fix whatever problem came my way. These problems started small and as I would dwell on them they became increasingly complicated. I began to believe that the rest of the world would be a better place if I would contribute my humor and lightheartedness to it.

Being the only man of the house due to my father's absence I acquired a great deal of sensitivity for the two females that I was living with. My mother, for the most part, was very nurturing toward me, and Jennifer's attention was bliss when she would express it in a positive manner. My father would visit mainly on Christmas day for fifteen or twenty minutes, just long enough to drop off a gift for Jennifer and me. Because Jennifer and I would not hear from him for most of the year, we often felt excited that he was coming over on Christmas day. He would not stay very long; therefore, I often felt abandoned over and over. He would re-open the wound that I couldn't heal on my own. I couldn't make him love me. I couldn't make him stay. I had no control. Why didn't he want us anymore? I recall thinking of him as a stranger.

My mother dated when I was between five and twelve years old. I would often seek guidance from the men she dated. I thought of them as my male role models. One night when I was ten years old my mother went out on a date. I was working on my bicycle in my room. Jennifer was babysitting me. My mother was not gone ten minutes when Jennifer barged in and started beating me for no reason. I grabbed my kickstand and chased her. She locked herself in the bathroom. I was so angry that I beat a hole in the door with the kickstand. Jennifer came out of the bathroom to tell me how much trouble I was going to be in when my mother came home. When my mother finally did come home she was very embarrassed in front of her date, but I did not get into trouble. Instead what I got was an empty promise from her boyfriend about how he was going to take me fishing. I was really let down when I realized the promise was never kept. It's obvious now that he was probably just a nice guy trying to be kind to a kid with no dad.

My mother's boyfriends were not the only father figures I would cling to for security as I grew older. Older boys, uncles and even male schoolteachers would become guides that I would constantly scrutinize to fill the void that was created when my dad and mother split up. I found it difficult when I was in school to hear about other fathers taking an interest in their children when my father was absent from most of my life. There were times when I was asked by schoolmates what I was doing for the weekend. So many times I wished that I could respond for just one weekend by saying that my dad and I had plans. Looking back now I can honestly say that I was giving hope to a hopeless situation. My mother had to play both roles of mother and father. I know that this was not easy for her to do and I am sure that she felt a great deal of strain, pressure, and an overwhelming sense of responsibility for both Jennifer and me.

When I was eleven years old I began working out with weights for two primary reasons. First and foremost I believed that I needed to be strong in order to protect myself from outside threats. I also thought that I needed to protect my family from threats that may yet come. All of the gloom that the world had to offer is what I found myself trying to combat. What was wrong with this equation is that I never put much thought into not being a bully, nor did I ever think to let the world save itself. As I grew older and more educated I learned to talk a good talk in order to avoid the fistfights. Although my bullying at school subsided, I still had this fantasizing idea that I could make a great difference in the world.

When I was eleven years old, my mother, Jennifer and I moved to the Westbank of New Orleans. We moved there because our neighborhood was deteriorating and my mother wanted to be closer to her mother and two brothers. She moved during the summer while I was at camp and I came home to a two-story house, which made me feel rich and popular. We moved from a one-story house on the east side of town where crime was flourishing. The new house was a fresh start for me. When compared to where we were as to where we had moved to, it was like better schools for Jennifer and me, and new friends and fresh opportunities for all three of us. At age thirteen I got into skateboarding. It was the new thing to do. Of course I got hurt and was always hanging out in the street. This sport helped me to become very popular among my peers. One summer my friends decided to take up a collection for a new ramp for us to skate on. I only had fifty dollars and I had just ordered a new skateboard deck from California. The company was going to send it cash-on-delivery and my mom agreed to pay for airmail on her credit card. When the board arrived, the deliveryman said that it had all been paid for. Apparently they charged everything to my mom's credit card. Once that happened I gave my friends the fifty dollars to build the new ramp. When my mom received her credit card bill, she wanted the money for the board and I told her that

I gave it to the deliveryman, which was a lie. I went to camp that summer with my new skateboard oblivious to what was happening back home. Back home my mother had contacted the postal service and there was a big investigation about where my money had gone. When I returned home a detective called and asked if I would come to his office and give a description of the postal worker who took my money. I had to confess as to what happened and I was reprimanded accordingly. I learned that tampering with the mail is a federal offense punishable by prison time. I realized that I got off easy because I was a kid but I might not be so lucky if there is a next time.

My uncle owned a restaurant and he gave me a job when I was thirteen years old. I began making money while going to school. The money I made helped me buy cigarettes and Zippo lighters which enabled me to keep my cool image around my friends and family. Sure, some said that I should quit smoking, but to those I felt like a rebel. I was twelve years old when I started smoking cigarettes to be cool. I believed that people would like me better if I smoked. I saw images that would relate to my habit such as the Marlboro man and the Joe Camel cartoon character. My depression became hard to handle as I grew older and these characters were no longer cool to me, however, I continued to smoke because it felt good and I believed that I needed it as a crutch. This crutch would consume my lifestyle to the point that I believed that I could not function without cigarettes. I now realize it's the price I paid for trying to fit in with society and to be cool with my peers.

I recall another mishap when I was thirteen. I began horsing around with a survival knife at a friend's house. I had it in my grasp by the handle and my friend grabbed the blade. As a reflex and in an instant I pulled away and sliced his hand open. His wound healed and not long after he decided that he wanted me to have the knife. I kept it for a while then sold it to another friend who told me years later that he had to use the knife in self-defense. According to him, he was riding his bike one night to his girlfriend's house when a stranger approached him. The stranger tried to steal his bike so my friend stabbed him several times with the knife and left him to die. He was not sure if he killed the perpetrator but he did say that he tossed the knife in a canal. This awful knowledge made me feel two emotions. Happy the knife helped my friend but sad for the guy he stabbed. Even at age fourteen I knew that a bike was not worth someone's life.

I was a friend with another guy who was always in trouble. Whether he was skipping school or stealing from the corner store, trouble was not unfamiliar to him. I remember getting off of the school bus one afternoon and shell rocks were breaking all around me on the bricks of my house. I looked across the street and there he was with a slingshot. Apparently I was choosing dysfunctional friends. Perhaps this was my comfort zone.

In dealing with the sexual encounters that I experienced between the ages of eight and twelve, I came to question my sexuality for years. The babysitter who attempted to seduce me made me feel cool and macho. This stroked my ego nicely even though I still did not have complete understanding of exactly what had taken place. However, the molestation by the camp counselor made me feel very uncomfortable with a great deal of fear and skepticism that lasted into much of my young adult life. The fact that I got an erection when he sexually abused me caused me to question my sexuality. Was I gay? I was still attracted very much to women. This doubt caused a great deal of anxiety. It would not be an understatement to say that I had a lot of developmental issues that needed to be addressed.

The reason I began going to summer camp was so that I could make the most of the summer and to give my mother a break from raising children. At this particular camp, I would meet girls on the train as well as at the campsite in Tennessee from the time that I was around ten until I was fifteen years of age. One girl that I recall was truly the prettiest girl in the camp and because she liked me, other campers were jealous. One night before a dance, I was getting ready and while in the shower, a camper came to the shower house and took my towel. We would walk from the shower house to our cabins after taking showers and because my towel was stolen I had to streak back to the cabin completely naked.

When I got to the cabin the screen door was locked. When the boys in the cabin finally unlocked the door, I went in and received a terrible whipping from six or seven rat-tails. This is when someone wraps a towel and rolls it tight. They began whipping these towels as hard as they could all over my body. I began to fight the biggest guy in the cabin. Once I got the upper hand, everyone left. Needless to say I wanted to run away from the camp and return to New Orleans. Unfortunately, I would remain at the camp until the session was over. I had to grow up quickly, learn to defend myself, and stand up for whatever I believed in at an early age. I felt I had to over-compensate for my small size.

One developmental issue that stands out is in relation to security and trust. As I developed into a preteen, my thoughts pertaining to females would fluctuate. Sometimes I felt secure in my relationships with my mother and sister. But in relationships with girlfriends, I experienced hurt and abandonment throughout the years. I felt much pain because of my sensitivity and openness toward those that I thought that I was in love with. The problem was that I had high emotions and anxiety that I would interject into those relationships. It was as if every girl that I dated since the first grade, in my mind, appeared to be the one that I would spend the rest of my life with. I attribute these thoughts mainly to my relationship with my mother who was overly protective of me. I felt as though I could confide in her and trust her with my life. The pain came when I got involved with girlfriends and could not understand that they were not interested in having me confide in them, nor were they willing or able to make me feel the security and trust that I was so accustomed to with my mother. Although my mother displayed a single parent full of worries and consumed herself with depressing thoughts, she did manage to provide me with peace of mind that she would take care of me and be there for me. It became apparent to me that the difference between a boy and a man surfaced after the boy had been kicked around long enough by several relationships with girlfriends. I finally realized that the man could stand alone without his mother or women. The downside is that by the time I figured this out and had been through the wringer with failed relationships that eventually left me debilitated and exhausted, I spent years trying to put the pieces back together.

I earlier mentioned that I received the "All American Camper Award" at fifteen years old. In order to achieve this award you had to work your way through a "Master's Program." The camp was split up into two sessions. The first session was from June through July and the second was from July to August with one week splitting the two. Each session was for a month long, and if you could afford it you could go for both sessions. There were many campers that only went for either the first or the second session, but from ten years old until I would be fifteen I was headed to Tennessee for many summers.

The Master's Program was an effective way of showing the campers development in the various activities and skills in which the staff and administration taught. It was comprised of several degrees of advancement in all activities in which the camper shows interest, skill, and sustained effort. Campers had choices of activities in which to specialize, and were to go to their chosen fields several periods each day. The Master's Program consisted of nine activity departments: Water Front, Sailing, Athletic, Tennis, Horseback Riding, Crafts, Riflery, Archery, and the Wilderness.

The degrees of advancement were set up by the department heads. The camper could only meet these requirements by sustained effort through specialized instruction. A normal daily schedule for a camper was: 7:15-Reveille; 7:45-Breakfast; 9:00-Choice of Activity; 10:15-Period of Scheduled Activities; 11:30-Master's Program, Swim Period; 1:00-Dinner; 2:00-Rest Period; 3:00-Period of Scheduled Activities; 4:30-Afternoon Swim Period; Choice of Other Activities: 6:00-Supper; 6:45-Vesper Service; 7:00-Usually a Free Period for all campers. On certain nights special camp programs such as two picture shows weekly, dances and parties, Council Ring, Kangaroo court, a County Fair, etc.; 9:15-Taps.

There are three degrees of advancement in each deparment. For example, in Horseback Riding the camper must first become a Horseman in order to receive a "First Degree Certificate" in

Horseback Riding, then a "Master Horseman," and finally a "Distinguished Horseman," by exhibiting sufficient skill, ability, and interest. Time is of course an element in obtaining these awards. Beautifully designed brassards are given for each degree of advancement.

In addition, to become a Master in any field, the camper must have shown a fine general camp spirit of loyalty, cooperation and sportsmanship, as judged by the masters committee of counselors. Receiving the first Master, the camper is inducted into the order of the Cumberland's in an impressive ceremony at the Council Ring.

When a camper receives a master in three fields of endeavor, one is awarded the degree of MASTER CAMPER, a signal honor. To become a DISTINGUISHED CAMPER, one must become distinguished in one field and have four other Masters—a great accomplishment which requires several summers at camp and in order for me to receive the highest honor of the Master's Program, being that of "The All American Camper Award," I went to this particular camp in Tennessee for two months each summer for five years. I earned six Masters, three Distinguished, and nine First Degrees. Finally, I was on top of the world. I was the best at many things compared to a large number of peers! Little did I know that I would soon have to deal with mortality issues.

Later that same year I received a phone call. My aunt called to say that one of my in-laws committed suicide in a Texas hotel room. I froze when I heard the news. This man just married my cousin not long ago and they had a beautiful baby. When we went to the wake, the baby was not allowed to see his dad in the coffin because his family was afraid that he would ask his dad to hold him and start crying when his dad did not respond. I was fifteen years old and this was the first wake that I had ever been to. I recall the make-up that covered the entrance wound from the impact of the bullet like it was yesterday. I stood over his body and thought that all I had to do was stick my finger through the make-up and I would be inside of his skull. I know that this really sounds morbid but I was really freaked out. From then on his family would release balloons up into the sky on his birthday. His child would say, "My daddy lives in the sky." As I grew older I came to realize how precious life is and the difference that one life can make.

These early life and preteen experiences really had me frightened, confused and unsure about the quality and length of my own life. I was constantly on guard, skeptical and on the defense in whatever I did. I lacked the guidance and knowledge that I would later acquire to help pull me through. But, in the meantime, I felt alone to deal with all of my bottled up manifestations and inhibitions. It would become of no surprise that I would begin to take risk and push the envelope in all that I did if for no other reason than to feel as though I was living life to the fullest.

Chapter 3

Adolescence

The mixed ups and downs of adolescence
Teenage pregnancy and the social stigma

Coming into adolescence at the age of thirteen many issues arose regarding safety and security. My mother was constantly worried that something bad might happen to Jennifer and me. Her insecurities would eventually rub off on us. I did not feel safe. I found myself working out harder with weights and I was acting tough when I did not need to. My tough guy persona was how I hid my fears. I felt as though any issue that arose within the bounds of our family had to be sorted out or solved by me. When I began working at a restaurant at thirteen years old any money that I made was to help my mother or sister in any regard. Often I felt as though the money would have to compensate for me not being there when problems would arise between them. Being the only male of the house, I felt subconsciously that I had to not only save them from the world but also from each other. My personal sense of security and trust faded. As a result I found myself in a world that I feared. I trusted no one.

My mother has always emphasized that having a job was a big deal. This always made me work very hard for a minimal amount of money. She believed that if an employer gave you a job, then he did you a favor. I later realized that the only favors that were being done were by me. At least I was finally working hard and making money. I was now at the age where peers wanted to know if I was having sex. These older peers were role models for me in the absence of my dad. I soon became inundated with pressure to have sex so that I could belong and be like my sexually active peers. Sex became a driving force that filled me with excitement.

I began dating at age fifteen. This particular summer I was working at the neighborhood car wash with my friend Josh. I was making minimum wage plus tips. I had no real responsibilities so the money I made was used as expendable cash. I felt rich. One day Josh and I were working at the car wash and in walked this beautiful girl. She was tall, had big brown eyes, a shapely body and long brown hair that framed her face and cascaded around her shoulders. To my surprise Josh knew her and I told him that I had to be introduced to her. Her name was Paulette. He and I made plans to go out that night and he agreed to bring her along. I wanted to go somewhere where I could get the chance to get to know her. I had to know this girl. Later that night me, Josh and Paulette went to a pool hall and shot pool. The beer was cheap and Bon Jovi was spinning on the jukebox. The year was 1988. We shot pool at the bar and walked down some railroad tracks until we reached a park. We sat on bleachers and talked for a while until it was time for us to go home. The next day I got her number from Josh. As the days passed I began to fall for her and the attraction became mutual. We would talk the nights away and we seemed to connect. Before we knew it we were now dating for three months. Paulette and I were both fifteen years old. One evening while at her mother's house we were making out and things went too far. It was the first time either one of us had sex. We had only been dating for three months and Paulette conceived with that first sexual encounter. No one mentioned anything about birth control and if they did I never understood completely because I was not given enough information about it. We were both virgins. She was scared to death and the pregnancy consumed our every waking moment. What were we going to do? I told her that I would stay with her no matter what she chose to do. We continued to engage in sexual activity in spite of the pregnancy on a regular basis and both of us were inseparable.

Three months had passed, six tests had been taken and every one had been positive. Paulette was definitely pregnant. It was time to tell our parents. When she told her mother she became furious. In time her mother came to accept and deal with the situation. My mother was not happy at all and did not want this to interfere with my education. She did not want me to marry Paulette and even brought up the idea of abortion. I reassured Paulette that I would stay with her no matter what she decided to do and that the decision was mainly up to her because it was her body. I also told Paulette that her education was important and I did not want to see her drop out of school. Paulette told me that her mother could stay home with the baby while she finished high school. We decided to have the baby. I felt bad about what happened but there was not a minute of the day that passed that

I did not think about Paulette and the baby. I was still in high school and living with my mom. Many people find teen pregnancy a focal point for criticism and failure. I chose to look at it as a challenge and a source of growth that helped to enable me to conquer average problems with the greatest of ease. Anyone could walk away from a problem and there were times when my family wanted me to. At age fifteen people were telling me to leave her behind, but I knew that she did not get pregnant by herself and I decided that it was time for me to be a man and face my responsibilities. The idea of more responsibility was much more appealing than the actual reality. I knew Paulette's family was poor. She had three brothers and three sisters. She was the youngest of the three girls and had one younger brother. She was the sixth child. Her dad was a painter and her mother was a stay at home mom. They lived in a one-story four-and-a-half-bedroom house. They had to relocate many times due to late rent or for having too many people living in the house or apartment. I cared for Paulette regardless of her families' status. I felt in comparison that I was from an upper-middle-class family. My mother's dad was a grocery store owner. He made a very good living back in his days and was able to leave the store's property to my grandmother when he died. This property was located in a prestigious part of town and quickly became prime rental property for my mother and her two brothers when my grandmother passed. When my dad walked out of our lives my mother kept the house they were buying together. It was a double so my mother rented out the other half, which helped her to pay the bills. She soon found a job as a secretary. We eventually had enough money to relocate to the Westbank into the huge, two-story home I'd lived in since age eleven. The old house became 100-percent rental income for us. With my mom working, the rental property and our big house I did feel rich as I mentioned earlier.

Although I knew Paulette's family was less fortunate I saw something special in her and I loved her no matter what our differences. It was obvious that everyone was having trouble making ends meet and emotions ran very high everywhere we went. Paulette and I had to assume total responsibility for the pregnancy and we always wondered how we were going to get through it. We tried to be optimistic about our future but we were never sure what was to become of the situation. Once we accepted the pregnancy and faced the fear of telling our parents we felt free to have as much sex as possible. Having sex became a form of refuge for each of us. When we went out friends did not even believe that she was pregnant because she always looked thin. Schoolmates were constantly inquiring about our popularity and us, as a couple seemed to be the talk of the town. It seemed as though everywhere we went we were constantly running into someone that one or both of us knew. The pregnancy would change our lives forever. Paulette's pregnancy lasted eight months and during that period of time we did everything together. We rebelled against our families. We had to grow up quickly, however, and be mature about our situation.

Paulette and I found ourselves being criticized by both family members and outsiders. My mother was the first to tell me that we were just "kids having kids" or that "You should just go get somebody else pregnant!" Paulette and I were consumed with anger and frustration. As time wore on we began to fight among ourselves. My education began to be the last thing on my mind and I felt too exhausted and beat down to care. I ended up failing tenth grade because I allowed this new situation to completely consume my every waking moment. I did not however, decide to drop out of high school.

On Monday, February 20, 1989, our son Holbrook was born. I missed the actual birth. I was in school repeating the tenth grade. When I found out that I was the father of a newborn infant the feeling of pride that I had was overwhelming. I was so proud of Paulette for going through all that she endured and for bringing a part of us into the world. Our son was beautiful. Paulette delivered in Charity Hospital due to the fact that we were without health insurance. When my son was being delivered the nurse accidentally inserted a heart monitor too deeply into Paulette and punctured my son's head. That puncture was the only mark on our child at the time of delivery. The doctors assured us that he would be fine. Holbrook was one month premature, weighed five pounds, one ounce, and was sixteen inches long. The principal of my high school allowed me to stay home the following day to spend time with Paulette and Holbrook in the mother baby unit at the hospital. My mother ordered premature diapers out of Chicago because the hospital only had so many. Once Holbrook came into our lives for the moment all of the tension and negativity subsided. When he arrived at home he went to live with Paulette's family. I was the first to change his diaper and everyone was so happy that he was home. There was a surprise baby shower where Paulette and I received many nice gifts with all of the trimmings that a baby shower could have. Everywhere we went people both friends and family made such a fuss over Holbrook. He was more famous than we could have ever imagined. I found myself riding my bike back and forth to Paulette's house to see Holbrook after school and after work to help as much as I could. I did not know the first thing about being a father. I often wondered what kind of father would I be and if it would be enough for Holbrook. The truth is that I did not even know how to hold an infant but once I learned I never wanted to put him down. The first infant that I ever held was mine and the first diaper I ever changed belonged to Holbrook. Paulette did most of the work because he lived with her. I felt responsible and somewhat guilty because I could not do all that Paulette did for Holbrook. Because of school and work I could not be there to share in all of the responsibilities all of the time like Paulette could. Not long after Holbrook was born and Paulette was able to start going out again, Paulette began to treat Holbrook like he only belonged to her and she soon began to push me out of their life. This approach would soon become her stance against me for years to come. My mother was happy with her grandson but quick to implant her negative connotations about the situation once again. She was quick to deliberately point out that when children are small so are the problems but as they get big they become big problems. All of the negativity, however, gave Paulette and I fuel to rebel against the adult persecution if not for us, for our innocent miracle. Most of the fighting did subside because both families came to adore this new little addition to the family. Soon love replaced all of the bickering.

I had a job working for my uncle but the pay did not cover our expenses. Paulette began receiving government assistance such as "Women Infant Care" as well as welfare. She was trying her best and I was very proud of her. Any extras, however, would have to wait.

At the hospital Paulette did not put my last name on Holbrook's birth certificate. Instead Paulette gave our son her last name and claimed that the father was unknown. She did this for two reasons. The first reason she says was because she did not think that she would qualify for government assistance to help with the wellbeing of her and Holbrook. The second reason was because my mother thought that the courts would make me quit school and start working full time to pay child support. At that time, if I wanted to change Holbrook's last name to mine, I was told by the courts that I would have to adopt my own son. This did not make any sense to me and I was completely out of luck without Paulette's consent. [This was the Louisiana law in 1989; however, ACT NO. 834, Senate Bill No.177, Effective 7-2-99 (b) it was changed to be: If the child is acknowledged by the natural father and there is a plan for support then that child's surname "shall" be that of the natural father. This explains that the mothers consent is unnecessary under these conditions (unless the mother and the natural father agree otherwise). This, however, does not imply that support and visitation go together. Support, if not together, is an obligation; visitation is a right. Just because you pay child support does not give you the right to visitation. They are two separate entities.]

When it was time for Paulette to go back to school, her mother was in search of employment for her. She was no longer available to watch Holbrook. She found a job scrubbing floors and Paulette had to start staying home to watch our son. As soon as Paulette missed enough days of school she was dropped from the ninth grade. Her mother soon quit her new job. It became apparent to Paulette that her mother took the job because she did not want to watch the baby. Spiteful reactions came from everywhere. Taking on this type of responsibility was more than I could have ever imagined.

One day Paulette and I had an argument over the phone. Her twenty-six-year-old brother got involved in our argument and after she and I made amends he still had a grudge against me. He soon picked a fight with me and his mother broke it up by swinging a butcher knife between us after punches were thrown. It was definitely a dangerous situation for all of those involved. This was one example of the tension between both families.

Being sixteen with a child proved to be very difficult. There were many opportunities that were left by the way side because of new responsibilities. The responsibilities made me feel very important and I found myself always looking for the positives to come out of what appeared to be a doomed situation. As months went by Paulette's feelings for me changed. She had a friend who was constantly trying to introduce her to other guys and my friends wanted more of my time as well. Eventually our own jealousy and inside insecurities turned inward on us and we would fight. She became possessive with our son and treated me as an intruder, an outcast. It soon became evident that our son was hers to keep and I was just an outsider. She began saying that she did not want our son to be in my car without her because she did not like the way that I drove. No matter what I did I could never be trusted in her eyes with our son. I cannot express the intense pain that I was experiencing. Our two families squabbling also tormented me emotionally and it appeared that whatever I did was never good enough. I tried to keep peace for my son's sake but with Paulette's negative attitude toward me, I was always on the verge of being banished from my son's life. It would be an understatement to say that I felt as though my son was stolen from me and ripped out of my life. It seemed that Paulette and I could not weather the storm and stay united under such grave adversity. Juvenile Court would soon be the only option for trying to resolve the situation.

While my classmates were out drinking on weekends and going to concerts, I was home changing diapers or working. During the week, while classmates were home sleeping and getting rested for the next day at school, I was up at four o'clock in the morning warming bottles to put my son back to sleep. One thing that helped to ease the strain was our extended family. It was our families that provided us with the entire baby's needs: crib, bottles, clothes, etc. The help from our relatives and friends helped our emotional, financial, and physical support to strengthen; however, animosity was always just around the corner. Paulette and Holbrook lived with my mother and me for six months while I was still in high school. One-night things got so ugly between Paulette and I that Jennifer stepped in and beat up Paulette. We were at a bar and Paulette was breaking up with me for someone else. Jennifer was bartending at another bar next door. I went to soak my misery with Jennifer and she felt bad for me and against my wishes picked a fight with Paulette. I really did not know where to turn because of the violence that was mounting between my family as well as Paulette's family. There were times when it appeared as though everybody had an axe to grind with everyone else. Paulette and I were definitely growing apart. Being as young and immature as we were, the strengthened support was not strong enough to carry us through the coming years of college.

After graduating from high school I would later attend college where I found this article to help validate the positives in my situation for which I was yearning for so long. The article was written by: Geronimus, Arlene T. "Teenage Childbearing and Personal Responsibility: An Alternative View." Political Science Quarterly, Fall 1997 v. 112 no.3, pp. 405-431. In this article I realized that the issues involving teenage pregnancy range from a moral aspect to the socioeconomic aspect within societies, and all aspects in between. There is much negativity in the mainstream of American culture that looks down on the issues of teen pregnancy for all aspects, but a different and more positive approach to these issues is what appears to be the focus of the source that I used in this annotated bibliography.

Within the article, a lot of the negativity stems from misleading traditional morality and social oppression. The irony is that this misleading oppression is what often causes situations such as teenage pregnancy instead of the teen pregnancy as the cause for the social ills. There exists strong data that promotes the notion that risks such as low birth weight and infant mortality are lowest when the delivering mothers are in their mid to late teenage years of life. There is evidence that shows that the older the mother, the greater the risk for her first born child and the risk are highest in poor communities. Mortality rates for infants born to teens are twice as low as those delivered by older mothers within the community. The teens' infant is twice as likely to have a good birth weight compared to an infant born to a twenty-five-year-old mother and one-third as likely as an infant born to a thirty-five-year-old mother.

Just because a child is born to a teen does not mean that the child's development has a greater chance of being hindered when compared to children that were not born to teens. A teen's child can also make achievements in life that are not necessarily negative. In a national study of minority children, their performance on the Peabody Picture Vocabulary Test showed no correlation between the performances of a teen's infant's results when compared to that of an older mother's infant. With regard for infants born to white teenage mothers, the results are humble at best when compared to the large outcry for this public concern. There is even evidence of positive effects that surfaced among children who were born to teenage mothers that were between 18-19 years old at the time of delivery. These children that were studied ranging in age from 4-14 years old outperformed other infants whose mothers were older at the time of their delivery. The increase in performance was shown primarily with reading, math, and the Childs verbal ability. These findings are also shown when the teen group is compared to young teen mothers who are less than eighteen years old at the time of delivery.

In reference to the social stigma of teenage pregnancy, it is very easy to refer to it as negative. To see the parents as "kids having kids;" to see the child as a "mistake," and to focus on the parenthood as one without a father that consists only of a problem-prone immature girl who is raising her <u>unwanted</u> baby alone. It is this image that stands and screams out that the child's physical and psychological health are in danger and it is society that will pay the ultimate price. These same images would greatly ease if we restructured the image to represent the literature and the statistics that we have about the issue. According to statistics, two-thirds of teenage mothers are between 18-19 years old and forty percent are married. Most would also prefer to rely on their extended family from both maternal and paternal sides to aid in the support and nurturing of their young. When concerning ourselves with extended family functioning rather than a marriage form, it becomes evident that in some circumstances a greater stability, more care, and a stronger economic support for the child increases than when we place only a high value on a legal marriage. Sometimes the broken happy home is better than the unbroken unhappy home.

It is not always beneficial to assume that teenage pregnancy is caused by the abandonment of personal responsibility, but possibly, for the structured scenario mentioned in the previous paragraph. Such scenarios may consist of collaborations between the teens and elders in the making rational and responsible decisions for the psychological, physical, emotional, and financial stability for both the parents and the child. When looking at teen pregnancy in terms of teen priorities and society, it may be advantageous to see the priorities of those teens may indeed represent society. It is their bottled up manifestations that take on different forms to suit the situations that must be addressed. This scenario suggests that teen childbearing can sometimes be a health conscience economic strategy that may include but not be limited only to welfare generosity. It very well may be considered because of economic uncertainty that stems from many sources within the realm of life.

Some have suggested that teens have children for more independence through government programs. This only contradicts itself by the dependence on welfare. Instead of this carrot-stick suggestion, it may be that teens that are faced with this trade-off may actually encourage reduced welfare benefits if the child is born healthy and has able-bodied providers to be there throughout his childhood.

High rates of teen childbearing may not come from the sexual increase in teens primarily, but may encourage such behavior from external sources such as educational systems, labor market opportunities, child care, housing, and health. Any one of these alone can impede productivity, and shorten the lives of people who are young as well as those who are middle-aged and elderly. These anxieties may in turn push responsible future-oriented and caring adults in the direction of forming elaborate systems for social insurance, which exerts pressure on earlier childbearing and away from marriage.

I found this source to be purposeful in many different aspects in relation to the topic of teenage childbearing. It gives a deeper look into possibilities that are often never considered that give better understanding in regards to this type of behavior. It also shows how positive results can and do come out of what appears to be on the surface a negative situation. The source is also useful in pointing out that the external sources are what can often determine the road that people end up on and not necessarily the sources from within themselves. In addressing such external sources, this source could be somewhat of a crude map to begin a quest to identify the external sources that cause such negative anxiety. In reflecting on the relationship that I have with my son, it became a driving force for me to attempt to enhance not so much the quantity of time that we spend together but instead the quality of that time. Being on the outside of the relationship when compared to his mother's innermost sanctum with him made it very difficult at times to have some, if any, real relationship with him.

Paulette and I never married, although I did sign an Act of Acknowledgement stating that Holbrook was my son. Child support was established, and I fought for visitation. I was able to explain the situation as best I could for Holbrook and to be there if and when he needed me. I found that just showing an interest in whatever he did went a long way, which constantly reinforced our relationship. The article that I researched gave validation to what I had been suffering with all along. I believed in my heart that doing what was right from the onset of the pregnancy could only give way to great rewards. Even though I do not see Holbrook nearly as much as his mother does, a relationship does exist between him and me. There were many times that I was told how badly I screwed up. However, all of the negativity from friends and family made me fight harder because there were many times that I believed that it was just us against the world.

Chapter 4

Early Adulthood
Drugs and Family support

Once I finished high school it was time to consider what I wanted to do with my life. I had several options available to me and the decision for me was to either join the Marine Corps or go to college. With the Marine Corps I would have to leave home and possibly be stationed away for long periods of time. I decided against it mainly because of my new family as well as my strong commitment to furthering my education. I looked at several colleges and I decided to go to a school in Southwestern Louisiana. It was a big decision to make but I chose Southwestern primarily because of its academics as well as the distance, which was approximately two and a half hours from home. Because my family as well as Paulette's family were constantly squabbling, I decided that the school was far enough away so no one could just show up at my door, yet close enough that I could get home in case of an emergency. My plan was to get established as soon as possible, leave the two squabbling families behind and take care of my responsibilities with my new family away from New Orleans. I always strived to do well in school. School, for me, was an escape from a turbulent home life.

As I began going to college, my plan was to leave Paulette and Holbrook home in New Orleans until I got established enough to take care of them. Then I would attempt to bring them both with me and live our own lives away from the two squabbling families. The reality was that it was going to take quite a while and it proved to be very difficult because of the distance. Over time life began to become more difficult. Friends went separate ways, and before I knew it, those that once lent an ear began to turn away. Having a lot to say and no one to turn to, I began to realize that my emotions were running high while isolation and anger set in.

At college I found myself in the company of new friends, and I began experimenting with harsh drugs and binge drinking. I initially started to take drugs and drink to fit in with the crowd, however as time went on I found myself wanting and needing the substances to fill a void that began to surface with the absence of Paulette and Holbrook. There were times when I felt on top of the world and then there were times when I felt that the more friends I had the more trouble I was accumulating. I found myself spending more and more time alone. Anxiety began to set in. The lack of finances created additional strain. I felt as if I should not be in college but instead I should be back home in New Orleans working to support my girlfriend and son. Because of this, among other reasons, I was constantly driving the highway to either see my mom, Jennifer, Paulette or Holbrook. I was driving back and forth from school to home and back to school. I really began to lose myself in the midst of the chaos.

Back home Paulette was becoming restless and confused. In my absence she started going out. She met a guy named John at a nightclub. This was the turning point in our relationship. To my dismay she decided to move on. She believed that the fact that I chose to go away to college told her that she was not more important.

I had no choice but to move on with my life as well. This was the last thing that I wanted to do. I wanted more than anything to take care of Paulette and Holbrook. Paulette had the control now and I was completely out of control.

I met several girls while attending college, but because my heart was still with Paulette I initially did not pursue them. I had a lot of hope that Paulette and I would somehow work things out. I met many women both in college and in the nightlife back home. I was constantly going out to bars. After a while some of the girls back home would become very clingy. Although it made me feel good, I was still very jaded because of the loss that Paulette and I had endured. Paulette's new boyfriend and I did not get along at all. He and his family were all too eager to try to take over both Paulette and my son's life. One weekend I came home to New Orleans to spend time with Holbrook. Holbrook was approximately three years old at the time. I took him to a movie and he asked if he could spend the night with me. I called Paulette and she told me to come pick up some of his clothes. When Holbrook and I arrived at her house, John wanted to talk with me. I took a walk with him and he wanted to know why I was calling Paulette's house at midnight. I told him that Paulette and I have a child together and if I woke him up I apologize. At this point he told me that it was futile for me to visit my son because he was Holbrook's dad now. I refrained from fighting with him because Holbrook was in the car waiting for me. When I got Holbrook home Paulette called to tell me to feed him. I told her John was attempting to interfere with my visitation rights and that I would go to court to enforce my rights if I had to. She immediately decided that she was coming to get Holbrook from my house and that I was not going to be able to spend time with him. She didn't appreciate me threatening her with the courts. When Paulette and John arrived I called the police. John would not even get out of his car. I told the police what he said about being my son's dad. The police asked him what he meant by that comment and John said that he had been raising Holbrook for the past three months. The policeman told John that he did not care if John had been raising Holbrook for the past twenty years. Holbrook did not have his blood or DNA and he would never be my son's father. At that point I told Paulette and John to get off of my property and I took Holbrook inside with me to sleep over. The next day Paulette called to tell me that she and John broke up and she wanted to get back together with me. We would get back together until I would leave for college. She was seeing John and I off and on depending on who she wanted to be with at the time.

While away at school I became withdrawn. This complicated my life more. Some of the girls that I dated once Paulette and I broke off our relationship were overly possessive. I began spreading myself too thin in all of my relationships as well as my academics with school. My circle of friends, including myself, had no money so all we were doing was having sex. After realizing the impact that sex can have on my life, I became very cautious and used protection when I had sex. There were many weekends that I would come home to spend time with my son. On these weekends Paulette would often break up with John to be with me. She would tell me that she had told John that she loved him but she was in love with me. She once told me that she told John that she was only using him to get over me and he said that that was fine with him. As soon as I returned to school they would be back together again. She was having trouble being alone and deciding what or whom she really wanted. Once I felt like I had lost her for good I felt as though everything I tried to do was in vain. I felt alone and depressed. My stomach was tied in knots. I felt like I was a trash bag filled with broken glass. She was in my guts and everyday life became hard work just to deal with my emotional and mental health.

As for my financial support while away at school, my mother would send me money whenever she could. I was working two, sometimes even three jobs while going to school full time, and yet I was barely surviving both financially and academically.

Being a single parent, it was not uncommon for my mother to panic and get overly excited if the slightest thing went wrong. I found myself doing the same thing. Much fear began to surface. I wanted to constantly fight for what I thought I should be fighting for and I wanted to run away all at the same time. These emotions along with the use of drugs are what often caused me to feel like I was on an emotional roller coaster. The drugs that I took varied. At times Marijuana was the drug of choice, especially if I was feeling very energetic, hyper and sometimes angry. I cannot say for certain that I was addicted to it because more often than not it made me very sedated and tired. I took LSD and cocaine mostly to stay awake for late night partying. I do not recall hallucinating while being on any of these drugs. The biggest problem psychologically was a slight sense of paranoia and the guilt that I was letting my family down. I was so accustomed to wanting and striving to please everyone else that my own life really did not mean that much to me.

After taking drugs for a period of time I began to feel worse than when I began using them for recreational purposes. I was old enough to know the dangers of taking drugs but young enough not to have the sense to care. So many people would tell me that I had my whole life ahead of me so I figured that I could use the rest of my life to correct my problem. There were nights when I took drugs and I felt really good, but then I would get really depressed because I knew in my heart that what I did was wrong and guilt would consume me. One night I took LSD, stayed locked in my room and cried for at least seven hours. I look back on this night and recall it as a night I practically lost my mind.

On a return trip home I ran into a high school friend that worked at a bar in New Orleans. I was there one night when I met Mikey. She was attractive and very sincere. We talked about college for a while and she told me that she lived with her parents. As the night wore on I offered her a ride home and she accepted. We began dating and talking on the phone. Mikey family was wealthy. During this time I was sharing a small apartment with my cousin. The apartment was in Southwestern Louisiana. I would stay at the apartment while attending college and working at a tennis racquet shop stringing tennis racquets. Mikey and I ended up calling it off after about a year. She was too clingy and I felt after all I'd been through that I needed my space. Mikey's parents understood the difficulties I was going through with trying to visit Holbrook, and they realized that I did not want to bring him home when I had him for my two week visitation and every other week end during the summer of 1993 because of Jennifer and my mother's constant fighting. Her family and my family always got along great and my mother and I remained friends with her parents.

In the spring of 1993 I was at one of my jobs working up at school toward the end of the semester when in walked my mother and Mikey's mom. The school semester was just about over and they asked me what my plans were for the summer. I told them that I planned on staying in my apartment where I had been living and would continue to work instead of coming home. Mikey's mom made me an offer to move into their home for the summer, and told me that her husband liked me so much that he had a house key made for me and would give me an alarm code to enter the house and leave as I liked. They said that it would be a perfect opportunity to spend the entire summer with my son away from all the squabbling. I accepted Mikey's parents offer and moved into their home. I stayed in Mikey's bedroom. I lived there for the entire summer. I was no longer taking drugs. I was working at my uncle's restaurant applying aluminum fiber coating to his shopping center roof where one of his restaurants was located. He paid me minimum wage and allowed me to eat lunch from the buffet. The paint was made of an oil base and I ruined a lot of clothes. Not to mention pulling the hair out of my legs for several weeks each day in the shower, until Mikey's dad turned me on to gasoline in order to get clean. Life seemed to be good though. I was staying in a beautiful home where there was no squabbling, was able to be with my son and had an okay job making some cash. Time seemed to fly by.

For once I was enjoying life without the use of substances. I was living in a healthy environment. Mikey's wealthy family lived in an affluent neighborhood. There was no fighting or bickering. Mikey's father would give me one hundred dollars per week allowance for doing little things like washing their cars, putting down stone and pressure washing at their home. The money was used primarily for fixing the body of the car that my grandmother donated to me when she was no longer able to drive. After I repaired and had help painting the car, I finally had reliable transportation for school and for Holbrook, and this was the first car that I ever owned. I was enjoying my stay with Mikey's parents. Mikey's mother was a great cook and her father was a great inspiration. It was a refreshing change for me. I stayed the entire summer with them. Mikey's dad was a great father figure for me. After having the car for a while the engine blew because of an oil leak that I was naïve about. Mikey and I never got back together as a couple; however, I remained friends with her and her family. Mikey's dad generously donated a company car that he owned to me that was in great shape; and I will always be grateful for that family's generosity at crucial times when I really needed help. By this time Mikey's family had done more for me than my own biological dad ever did.

After another semester in college I really wanted to move back home and go to college in New Orleans so I did. By the time I started my new school I had been clean of all drugs for at least one year and I had not smoked a cigarette in three months. I was previously studying taekwondo mixed with hapkido while in college for my physical education credits while at Southwestern. When I returned to New Orleans I continued to practice my arts.

I was working out with weights every day, and I got a full time job as a site technician with a video bingo machine company. In addition to school and work I was going out every time I got the chance. I felt very popular with the nightlife; however, I was no longer using drugs or getting drunk. It was more of a social event than anything else.

There were many nights when the partying would really get out of hand. Fistfights would happen on a regular basis and people that I knew and cared about began getting hurt. I started to experience insecure thoughts about life and the world. There seemed to always be bad news on the television and in the newspaper. There were nights when I had to pump myself up to go out; because I was so scared that I might really hurt someone and or go to jail.

It got worse than that. My mind started wandering with out-of-control thoughts. I would ponder on predictions by Notre Dames that the world was going to end in 1994 when the two world powers would come together in peace by a third-world country. It was in 1993-'94 when Russia started to become a democracy. In the 1980s the Cold War ended between the United States of America and Russia. They were the only two world superpowers, both having high nuclear arsenals. The U.S. being a democracy and Russia totalitarian, both having great militaries, espionage infiltrators and the rest of the world for their undivided attention. The world was always eager to play both countries to the middle, especially when it came down to any type of weapons, information, or treason for the sake of profit.

In 1991 the United States had already gone to war and beat the hell out of the very rich third-world oil country known as Iraq in the Middle East in operation Desert Storm. It is for the sake of profit, hate and greed that the "black market" exists, and in saying this, it would not be that far reaching for a 1993-'4 Russian democracy who is disarming, for an angry third-world rich oil country run by a dictator to get his hands on a nuclear weapon. I was raised Catholic and I believed that there would be a second coming of Christ. One thing that happened in 1993-'4 was that there was a standoff in Waco, Texas, with a man named David Koresh. He had followers who believed that he was Christ. The news on television showed him quoting scripture from the Bible without a Bible. There was a standoff that was initiated by the government against him and his followers at his compound. His followers consisted of men, women, and children. When the compound was attacked by the government and caught on fire, he and his followers were killed.

These are what I believed to be at that particular time major exterior factors that supported my belief that the world was coming to an end. I strongly believed that something had to be done for the sake of mankind. Instead of me going along for the ride and letting the world save itself, I believed that I had to be some sort of revolutionary and save it from its demise. This type of thinking gave me the greatest feeling of purpose that I had ever felt; however, it was too big of a responsibility for any human being and an over-exaggerated ego. To recap my life so far, I've experienced a broken home, step-kid/brother relationship, half younger sister that I never see, spending every birthday away from family from seven years old until I became fifteen years old, being molested at eight years old which started psychotherapy at nine, fondling by the babysitter, questioning sexuality into my teenage years, abuse by Jennifer, humiliated in fourth grade by an ex-nun, whipped by six or seven rat tails over a pretty girl at camp, made All American Camper Award, knife incidents among friends, played parts of bully and funny little clown to combat insecurities from a single parent upbringing, learned the ways of the rich folks and the ways of those not so well off, exposed to suicide in my family at a young age, and had a childhood pregnancy at the age of fifteen. The baby was born and his mother and I could not hold the relationship together. I've gone away to college and moved back home. I've dated off and on. I've experienced life with drugs and without. It is now at the age of twenty-one and on October 12, 1993, after already experiencing Holbrook tell me when he was three and a half to four years old that he has two dads; I'm his dad and John is his dad. In not wanting to add insult to injury I merely replied that "you are luckier than most kids, because most kids only have one dad." I took the Act of Acknowledgement down to Vital Statistics at City Hall and happily applied my long overdue name on his birth certificate.

Sling shooting forward I find myself consumed with grandiose thoughts that I am with a greater purpose than anyone around me. Around this time in 1994, it was when Paulette was still seeing John. She was still trying to bounce off of both John and me depending on her needs. She became pregnant for the second time and told me that it was my child. I would later come to find out this was a lie. I felt as though my life was a soap opera and I had to be some kind of superhero to keep all of my pieces together. I did not believe that I was the father. I recalled all of the negativity that arose when she was pregnant at fifteen with Holbrook, who was now five years old. It would be an understatement to say that I was deteriorating rapidly and fearing total collapse.

Chapter 5

The Breaking Point
Mislead perceptions, psychological testing, misdiagnosis,
overmedication, and the distorted effects of
taking the improperly prescribed drugs for the illness

As time wore on, I believed in my heart that Paulette's second child was not mine. It turned out that the second child belonged to John. Paulette soon gave birth to a baby boy that she and John named Cody. Not long after the baby was born Paulette and John married. Holbrook now had a new stepdad and inherited step-grandparents. Holbrook's new step-grandmother became very fond of him and wanted very much for him to be her grandson as well as Cody. Cody was Paulette's second child and John's first. Paulette and John divorced after approximately one year of marriage. She met another man within a year and became pregnant with his child. It became obvious to me that she was the one that had a problem with commitment. But she had no problem moving on with her life to new relationships and having children. At this point in her life Paulette had three children from three men before marriage to any of them. Eventually Michael and Paulette were married. Michael had two children from his prior marriage that lived with him. Paulette gave birth to Michael's third child. It was a baby girl and they named her Clarice. Surprisingly enough Michael and Paulette's marriage seemed to last. Three years later Paulette gave birth to their second child, a son named Paul. Holbrook now found him to be the oldest child of six and inherited a great deal of responsibility. With the added responsibility instead of greater support came a great deal of squabbling from the extended families. On Holbrook's visitation with me, he appeared to be stressed and as a result failed fifth grade. Paulette's multiple relationships and births had somewhat of an adverse effect on Holbrook. My hands were tied because Paulette had primary custody of Holbrook and I was just a bi-weekend dad. The lack of control in my son's life was taking a toll on me.

Meanwhile my life was pretty much the same in that I did not move on into a new committed relationship with anyone. At this point in my life all I cared about was getting my education and seeing my son when I could. Nurturing my relationship with Holbrook became my life's ambition.

It was at age twenty-one when I experienced a nervous breakdown, obviously a culmination of all that I'd been going through as well as a psychological break. It began one night when I was in a nightclub. All of a sudden I experienced a terrible pain in my head. It was the 17th of April 1994. The pain was so great over my left temple that I had to leave the club. Upon leaving, unexplained and bizarre thoughts started in my head. I would later discover that these thoughts are called ideas of reference. To give you an idea of what I'm talking about when I was driving in my car and a disc jockey on the radio said, "We dance better than you," a simple statement that was part of whatever he was talking about. I took this particular statement and I quickly assumed that he was talking about me. This was when the paranoia began to set in. After that it was as if every song on the radio played in conjunction with what I had been thinking and feeling.

I drove as far as I could to get out of the radio's range, hoping that they could no longer be able to read my mind. Finally I drove back home around one o'clock in the morning. I went straight to bed. The next day I went to work at the bingo hall. I began suspecting that people rigged the machines so that customers would win. I turned off the machines and left the bingo hall. I was fired because of this incident.

At this point I found myself without a job. I still had to pay child support. My life was quickly deteriorating. The ideas of reference would become worse as time went on. I began thinking that my phone was tapped and it was as if every word that I thought and said was being addressed by the public. One morning I was watching television and my mother walked in the room. As I turned to look at her, the television went off. When I looked back at the television it went on again. I totally freaked out. My entire head became full of sweat; my body was burning up, yet my hands were as cold as ice. I began crying because of the fear when I thought that if I did not watch television no one could watch television. I was so scared and yet I had been clean of all drugs for a year. I guess my life had become so complicated that I started believing that I was superhuman in order to keep it all together. This was the beginning of my grandiose thoughts that would eventually lead me to believe that I was not only a god but the most modern and powerful god of all times. The irony is that as powerful as I felt, I was aware of the fact that my life was out of control. My thoughts were paralyzed. I was experiencing two thoughts that negated one another being a god and having no control over my life.

I recall two incidents that happened in 1994 that induced grandiose thoughts in my head, which aided in my belief that I had some special power in changing the world. The first was at my son's first stepdad's house. I was explaining a plan for world peace and he told me that everything I said was being played on the television as we spoke. The second incident happened a few days prior when a friend invited me to go work out at a health club. As soon as we began working out, four guys came over and began competing with us. They said that they could lift more weight than we could. I felt very competitive. As the competition went on I noticed that my friend and I were lifting the same amount of weight as them. I was dressed in black jeans and penny loafers and everyone else was in shorts and tennis shoes, which was the normal gym attire. I debated that even with us being dressed in those clothes; we did the same amount of weight as the guys that were challenging us. The guys conceded and agreed that they had been beaten. I told the guys to do what they had to do and that my friend and I were leaving. They replied that they had no choice. I didn't understand what they were talking about. I believed they were scared that I could beat them at anything. I left the gym feeling stronger than ever. My grandiose thoughts were definitely taking over. I believed that I was un-stoppable. I believed only what I wanted to believe and anything else did not matter.

It all began in 1994. With a psychological break I developed a chemical imbalance, which is an imbalance of naturally occurring chemicals between nerve cells in the brain. The serotonin and dopamine are the two chemicals that were not level in my brain. Every time a thought crossed a synapse, which is where the serotonin and dopamine are supposed to be, and because of too much or not enough, the thoughts were altered and I would easily jump from topic to topic. I could not even trust my own thoughts. I was very in tune with fear and it was as if I would get signals of things that were going to happen seconds before they did. I was reading extremely too much into everything. Every click, every crack, every word, license plate, siren, cry for help, laughter, anything that happened on television, radio or movies was an elaboration of my life sent to me from my very own supreme thought process. I was suffering from major grandiose thoughts that were destroying my mind. I was never sure if it was the creative realm in my mind that opened things up for me, or if it was the beginning of enlightenment. Whatever, it was extremely frightening and real. My family saw an immediate change in my behavior and called a psychiatrist. I was so scared. I believed that I made people itch and made red lights turn green. I also believed that people in general were literally reading my mind. I thought that if I had positive thoughts then positive things such as world peace would happen. However, if I had negative thoughts or spoke of negative things, then people would die. I was on a real power trip and losing control by the minute. I was so scared of my own thoughts and so uncertain of my future that I was incapacitated to the point that I was simply afraid to do anything, let alone move. I believed that any movement or words that I aspired to create would be followed by judgment and heckling by peers, friends or foes and my credibility as well as efforts would soon turn into a joke. By this time I was literally standing in a world of fear, and the more pain and suffering I felt, the more comfortable I became with these emotions.

At this point my family brought me to the hospital to be admitted. The staff gave me pills to swallow the first night. I was in my room when I heard people yelling and cars speeding outside. I saw headlights flashing through my window. When I looked out of my window there were people on a rooftop below waving at me. I did not know what to make of it all so I went to sleep. I started smoking again while in the hospital and I believed that if I could get released from the hospital I would be the most powerful man that ever lived. I knew that whatever happened I had to live. While eating dinner in the hospital one day a patient punched me in my jaw and I fell out of my chair and onto the floor. He hit me for no reason, and I did not even hit him back because I was so medicated. On several occasions I would lie awake in bed at night and I would hear someone drop something that made a strange sound outside of my door. Within seconds afterward I would feel bugs burrowing under my skin. I fought it at first and every time that I tried to leave my room the staff would tell me to go to bed. I thought that I had to somehow bear it if I was to get out of the hospital and go home. I would many times hold my breath to the point of exhaustion and finally I would pass out. Life for me had become a living hell.

I was taking prescribed pills morning, noon, and night. I did not know what I was taking and if I refused to take the pills, they would give it to me in an injection. Little did I know the medicine would prove to be a blessing in due time for me. Days passed by and I was getting worse. My vision was blurry and I could not read without wearing glasses. The medication was not without side-effects. They finally administered laxatives to combat some of the problems caused from the medicine.

I spent thirty-three days in the hospital. They tested me for everything from drugs to lead and all the results were negative. I received and EEG and my brain activity was normal. I was soon diagnosed as paranoid schizophrenic. I had an MRI. The MRI showed no holes in my brain and all looked normal. I was taking between 50 to 55 milligrams of Haldol per day along with Klonopin and Zoloft. I later found out that a true schizophrenic that has the classic symptoms including holes in the tissue of his brain may require as little as 12 to 15 milligrams of Haldol per day.

I was originally diagnosed with having a paranoid schizophrenic mental illness. In 1995 I was re-diagnosed with a schizoaffective mental illness. This was not as bad as being schizophrenic, but still an illness of the mind just the same. Finally after getting a different doctor's opinion and having psychological testing done, a diagnosis that I more readily agreed with came to surface. The result was that of a schizoid type disorder, not a mental illness, but instead a personality disorder that I developed primarily in my teenage years. This meant that I could manage it with one on one counseling without the use of drugs and eventually outgrow it. At this point I was taken off of all of my medicine. I felt exonerated and redeemed. Because the medication had a side-effect of making me gain weight, once I was taken off of it I lost 55 pounds in a matter of two months. I began working at a courthouse and I went back to college in New Orleans. Unfortunately I had a relapse and had to be admitted into the hospital in the summer of 2000. The doctor gave me the bad news that the previous diagnosis of schizoaffective mental illness was correct. She prescribed Zyprexa, Klonopin, Neurontin, and one and a half CCs of Prolixin per month. Prior to that hospital stay and receiving the Zyprexa, Neurontin, and Prolixin, I was taking Risperdal. I would lie in bed for long periods of time, similar to the side-effects from the Haldol. The difference for me was that the Haldol made me sleep twenty-three hours per day. The Risperdal would make me tired all of the time, but I did find myself having the energy to get out of bed; however, once I got out of bed I would be exhausted again and have to go right back to bed. This cycle would repeat itself many times in a twenty-four-hour period.

In addition to my bizarre perceptions, the psychological testing, misdiagnosis, and overmedication there was also confusion and miscommunication between my mother and me. Every time my mother and I did not see eye to eye on certain situations she would tell the doctor that something was not right, there must be a better medicine, or that I was "off." One particular doctor adjusted my medication, which would take months for me to get used to. He said that there was no chance for rehabilitation. He gave the impression that we would have to learn to accept it and deal with it for the rest of our lives. There were times that I was so drugged on the medicine that I could not even speak to tell them what or how I was feeling. I was totally helpless and at their mercy. I can honestly say that my situation opened my eyes to what a medicational lobotomy must really feel like.

I was also diagnosed bipolar. This means that I suffer from manic depression. The depression for me often last longer than the mania and my actual diagnosis is schizoaffective. The affective is the bipolar (manic-depression) and the schizo represents the times when I became psychotic. The bipolar causes extreme lows as well as extreme out-of-control highs and I act and react like I am a paranoid schizophrenic, which includes but is not limited to the ideas of reference, paranoia, hallucinations, and grandiose as well as suicidal thoughts when my chemicals are not balanced and I go too high or too low. Sometimes the aforementioned happen all at once. When will I be well again, I constantly wondered?

Chapter 6

Rehabilitation

New doctor, Specialized Day Program, and the crutch of school

After becoming sick in 1994 my first psychiatrist claimed that no rehabilitation program was available and that I would have to spend the rest of my life on Haldol. This was the drug that kept me asleep twenty-three hours a day. Not the kind of news one would hope for. Upon eventually changing doctors, better medication was administered. I was now taking Risperdal. When I quit taking Haldol I experienced hallucinations for a short period of time. With Risperdal I was both energetic and exhausted all day long, but it was better than always sleeping. I was readily put into a specialized day program for rehabilitation. I was able to drive so I would drive myself to the specialized day program each morning and sit in on group sessions that consisted of patients, staff nursing and doctors. The sessions lasted from 8:30 A.M. to 2:30 P.M. Monday through Friday. This was where I began to interact with other people who had similar problems and were also on medication.

As time went on I began seeing myself become more involved with people around me. I began pushing myself to get better. My credibility, however, became torn once I went into the hospital facility. People would begin to say that I was crazy, sick, off, out of my mind and out of touch with reality. My new quest would be to find truth in all that I looked for. I found myself being totally honest in all that I said and did. If someone asked me a question I would divulge an answer that if under better judgment I would not have. This obsession with the truth stemmed from the grandiose thoughts that what I did and said had a profound impact on the world around me.

I didn't have to be consumed with affecting others' lives. I came to realize that I am but one man, a simple man with no special powers. In truth, therapy gave me structure. I made friends. I realized that it wasn't all about me. Therapy reintroduced me to the world again. With the medication and therapy I was slowly removed from my grandiose thoughts. I do at times still fight the thoughts to this day. Now I had to decipher what to do with me. Both family and friends had an idea as to what I should be doing with my life. Some would say that I was lazy and should go back to work, while others believed that I needed to rest. Every day was a struggle for me. I had good days and bad days. Because I would do something one day, people assumed that I could do the same thing every day. I would try to explain my different moods to people and my lack of interest in things. They just seemed to avoid me. As time wore on everywhere I turned up came another roadblock. So I quit turning and I let the roadblocks go on around me. Friends began leaving me alone, as they could not understand what was wrong with me, and I became very isolated from society because of shame and uncertainty.

Besides having a doctor that prescribed my medication, I had another doctor who would see me on a weekly basis to talk with me on a professional level about my situations, as they would arise. She had a master's degree in psychiatric nursing, and a doctorate in health education. I soon found out that she grew up with my mother. She allowed me to call her at any time as well as see her whenever I needed to. She was an important mediator between my mother and me. She helped me to realize feelings of security that I hadn't felt since I became sick. She helped me to speak about past behaviors and to reanalyze my thinking in order to learn and grow from them. She also assured me that if my mother and I had a disagreement that I would not be locked up in a hospital without having spoken with her and my other doctor first. Going back into the hospital was a real fear for me, so this reassurance allowed me to have a much-needed sense of calm in my mind. She began to teach me about my illness so I could understand more about what I was going through. We mainly fear those things that we do not understand. She was helping me to diffuse my fears by helping me to understand my illness.

One thing that she shared with me was her philosophy in life. It consisted of four C's, four T's, and four S's. The four C's consist of Care, Choice, Chance, and Change. The four T's consist of Truth, Trust, Try, and Time. The four S's consist of Safety, Security, Stability, and Solidarity. When combined, the lesson learned is: Care enough to tell the Truth for Safety. Make the Choice to Trust each other for Security. Take the Chance to Try for Stability. Change over Time for Solidarity. This helped put my mind at ease along with the building of trust in our relationship.

The specialized day program was the first program that helped enable me to get out of my house on a daily basis to establish structure. The group sessions helped me feel as though I could talk with people who were going through similar situations as me. We talked about situations that arose on a daily basis. It took away the feelings of being alone and isolated. For the first time I felt as though I did not have to battle my sickness by myself. The psychologist helped me to feel grounded.

I felt good enough to go back to school. I enrolled in the local community college. This proved to be another positive force in my life. When I began functioning at the college level again I really did excel. I earned an associate's degree in Criminal Justice, became a member of the Phi Theta Kappa honor society and made the Dean's List. Even though I had a mental illness, my intelligence and ability to learn was not affected.

I think of school as a crutch that I needed in order to give myself a new purpose. I felt purposeful to both instructors and schoolmates both on and off the campus. College did a lot for me and one thing that I will always be grateful for is the experience. College set me on the right road and showed me more than ever that I can do anything I set my mind to. In college I was around many people who did not know me, and they still treated me like I both mattered and belonged. This was one thing that gave me a feeling of confidence, helped me get my mind off of myself, and confirmed how important it is to take care of one another. I no longer was suffering from grandiose thoughts. It was with the help of other people that I was able to get my mind back, as well as realize how loving and kind others can be.

At this point in my life I was feeling positive about life again. I was coping with the fact that I had no control of my son's life. I had the mental break and got diagnosed and re-diagnosed. I was prescribed medications, both correct and incorrect. I survived therapy and the torment of being confined in the hospital. Now I was taking properly prescribed medicine and had my mother's childhood friend for a therapist. I completed a college degree. I now had a better understanding of my illness. The medication made me well and as functional as anyone else. Now the question for me became, how well am I, what can I do and cannot do, and what should I do?

Chapter 7

Medical Side-Effects and the Reactions of Others
Isolated only to be reintroduced (son, parents, siblings, peers, and doctors)

The sedated side-effects from my medication virtually stole at least five years of life from me. I had no quality of life. The medicine was really taking a toll on me both physically as well as psychologically. I say psychologically because although the medication was an anti-psychotic treatment, I still experienced side-effects such as anxiety, nervousness, and restlessness. Sometimes the only thing that I could do was lie face down into a pillow. Along with the Haldol I was simultaneously taking Zoloft, an anti-depressant. This made my mouth dry, and I was also taking Co-gentin; this was what made my eyesight blurry, and contributed to my restlessness. During all this time I still had visitation established with my son and I would be too exhausted to interact with him. I would buy him things to keep him occupied when he was young; however, as he got older he came to realize that all I did was sleep. Several times he would complain that he did not want to come over and just watch me sleep. The medication really did wear on my relationships with those closest to me as well as with my friends. I was told that during the first year that I was sick I did not even smile. I recall my left hand being paralyzed in the sense that I was only comfortable when my small finger and left ring finger were tucked into my palm.

While I was being nothing more than a zombie, my mother was stricken with concern and fear for my mental health. There was little she could do for me. She was my caretaker. She took me to my doctor visits and took me out to eat. She wanted me to get out and interact with people. She always told me that we were going to beat this thing. She was constantly trying to get my medication either changed or adjusted. My illness was taking its toll on my mother as well. Many times I would just gaze into the air and have my crazy grandiose thoughts. Somehow I think it was these grandiose thoughts that kept me from giving up and the irony being that the thoughts were a result of the sickness. My mother was helpless where I was concerned but not hopeless.

As I went through my post-psychotic depression, committing suicide was the main thing that I longed to do. The doctors were bringing me back down to earth and away from believing that I was a god. I was constantly depressed and everything that I thought I had built for myself had crumbled. When I finally hit bottom I realized, if for no other reason, I had to live for my only son.

There were many friends and family members who insisted that my son's birth was the gravest mistake that I had ever made. My reply has always been simply that a mistake is only a mistake when you never learn from it. I have always learned from my son both in person and in spirit. His presence has been a driving force for my existence in what at times appears to be a world of nothingness. As Holbrook was growing up he looked for guidance. I tried to give him what little knowledge I had in order for him to pick and choose what type of life he might like to have. It's funny how the age gap is only a difference of sixteen years, yet what I call teaching he still calls preaching. That tells me that I'm getting through to him. He has saved my life by just being there and he will always be my hero.

I cannot say for certain if the extenuating circumstances in my life caused me to get sick or if it was genetic. It very well may have been a combination of both. I say this because many people have the gene that can cause a bipolar personality but it many times does not manifest as mine did.

In looking into my family history, my father had a similar reaction when he was sixteen years old. Back then they strongly believed in shock therapy. He ended up receiving twenty-one shock treatments for depression; however, he was never put on medication and is functioning normally without it today.

Within the last year my father and I have begun to establish a somewhat amicable relationship. I cannot help wondering why it took us so long. As a child I thought that it might have been something that I did to cause the separation between us, but as an adult I suppose that he just did not want to be tied down with the added responsibility of kids. Regardless, I cannot condone his actions. He could never make up for all the years I had to grow up without a dad. He cannot reverse the pressure that was placed on me due to his absence. I knew that my son would never know this feeling of abandonment. I was in his life as much as his mother and the courts would allow me to be.

Many of my friends decided to go their own way and it seemed as though the only people that I had left to spend time with were my immediate family. No one really knew what to make of my situation. I was mostly alone, confused and often frustrated because of too much interfering information as well as the lack of information. People who were close to me began to undermine things that I would say. They acted as if what I had to say was either unimportant or just downright strange. I felt as though I was not being taken seriously and it would surface in my speech, actions and relationships. My son was five years old when I got sick. Most of his memories of me were during the time of my illness. As a result of people having lack of respect for me due to my condition, I had to combat the strain it posed on me in relation to raising my son. On several occasions when Jennifer would be visiting, she had a bad habit of encouraging Holbrook to sass me whenever I would tell him something. He wouldn't listen to her initially but eventually he would become disrespectful toward me. Another example of this lack of respect was when I told him to stop jumping on the sofa and to quit using perverse language. He ignored me so in my frustration with him I slapped him on the head to get his attention. He punched me with what seemed to be all his might in my jaw. This irritated my jaw, which began to give me TMJ problems. I grabbed him and threatened him in an attempt to control the situation. As time went on I began to feel helpless and as though I couldn't express myself. I acquired a temporary stutter as a result. Sometimes I think that if I had not gotten sick the way I did, a lot of adverse incidents would never have manifested.

Staying home is what often causes me to feel like a prisoner in my own mind. I find that I'm constantly reintroducing myself to people who came into my life. The medication often caused me to forget details to the point where I feel as though nothing is important. Maybe it's because I'm growing older and lost interest in things that I used to find interesting. There was a time in my life when everything was a big deal. I just can't capture those gleeful feelings anymore. I wonder if I ever will again.

Much time has elapsed from the day that I initially went into the hospital and was originally diagnosed. Throughout that time I have seen my son grow up, friends move on, siblings get married, and parents have become regular people to me. I look back on my twenties as the dark years because most of my time had been spent in bed sleeping. There was not much interest in doing what other peers my age were doing. Mainly because I felt like I had experienced so much more than they had. I felt beyond them in years. I completely isolated myself from society.

Chapter 8

Conclusion

That was then, this is now

The revelation of spirituality

Upon looking back on my life and all of the things that I have endured I find that I can take comfort in the proverbial "that which does not kill you will only make you stronger." In retrospect my life was engulfed in much adversity in only a small period of time. In the beginning I felt as though I had to be strong enough to hold everything together, however, the more I tried, the more things fell apart. After losing everything and being consumed in weakness and despair, my life continued with its ongoing changes. Perseverance is one thing that should never be underestimated. In doing this you earn wisdom and strength. There were many times that I found myself constantly second guessing each and everything that I did. As I now look back on my younger years in the midst of all of the chaos, I realize that I was never surer of what I was really doing until I began to live in the present. When I would ponder on the future or complain about the past I never lived in the present. This inability to appreciate the present kept me in a constant state of confusion and anxiety.

I began writing to find my own understanding about all of the situations that were mentioned throughout this manuscript. I realized that those situations were lived in a different time in my life, not in my present life. My life is now very normal, less chaotic and a lot less stressful when compared to the life I lived as a younger man. It borders boring when compared to all of the excitement of my teenage years. I have a greater sense of security and trust which enables me to feel safe wherever I go. I cannot help but recognize that all of the turmoil that I went through taught me what I really did not want to incorporate into my adult life. After the early pregnancy at age fifteen and the out-of-control relationship with Paulette I've found myself jaded and evasive of getting involved with anyone else. It's been many years and under normal circumstances anyone else would have had several relationships by now. I contribute most of my resistance to move on to the years of medicating myself with prescribed drugs. As I mentioned before, I slept much of my years away. The medication has greatly reduced my libido and I am not in need of sex like many other men. The low libido has allowed me to spend much of my time alone. Over the years I did connect with a female neighbor. We talk almost every day and have done so for the past eight years. She is much older than me but in many ways she fulfills my thirst for intellect. We talk about everything from my illness to religion. A turning point for me happened on November 30, 2003, when we were talking and she couldn't find the words to help me find my personal relationship with God. She was aware that my spiritual life was asleep and tried to help me reform my personal relationship with God. She gave me a bible and although I was eager to revisit my faith that my illness stole from me I was scared to read it in front of my mom. I feared that she would think that I was sick again and have me committed. My neighbor nonetheless tried to help me. It finally happened for me on November 30, 2003, when she said, "You just have to love Him with your heart, and you need to open your heart to Him. He's been with you all this time." What a revelation for me. The realization that I hadn't thought about my heart in years was astounding to me. The doctors never talked to me about my heart. They talked about my mind. Everything for so long revolved around my mind—losing it, medicating it, and thinking with it. I forgot about my heart. From fear to fantasy, pain to joy, and from illness to rehabilitation, all of these extremes have emphasized more than ever that God is in each and every one of us and to find Him is to find peace.

All of the therapy, mainly that which addressed my chemical imbalance, had put so much emphasis on my brain, my thought process, my mind clicking off and on and my racing thoughts that I was putting all of my energy into believing that I had to somehow figure my problems out cognitively. I realized in the course of the conversation that I needed God back in my life. I'd been so preoccupied with my mind that I stopped feeling with my heart. This was the day that I was awakened to the truth that God lives in my heart and it was I who left Him, not He who left me. Since November 30, 2003, I have never felt alone again or more at peace with the world around me. I have peace now that I know I do not carry my burdens alone. It's even better to feel consoled by a loving and merciful God. Since all of this began for me, I've survived it all. Now I know it was with the grace of God.

I thought I had to fix everything and everyone that was in need of fixing. That ridiculous misconception helped to promote my mental breakdown. It is God who fixes things and makes them right again. I am but a man. The best I could hope for is to find peace in this life and now I have. I am presently single and content. I am regretfully on disability. I always find myself going back and forth. Should I work, am I living off the system? The truth is that I can't work yet, so I have to accept the cards that have been dealt to me. We all have a cross to carry. The storms only make us stronger and wiser. We are never alone. Now I know it was His loving grace that carried me through this fearful ordeal. I am wiser. I am stronger. I have peace in my life and God in my heart. I am a better man for all of it. That was then...this is now.

Looking back in hindsight my personal hypothesis is that when a person's mind goes through enough trauma, whether it be stress and/or a genetic defect, the thought process of that person becomes permanently altered. The brain goes into abstract or unreal thinking patterns and can easily give way to schizoid behavior as a defense mechanism. My doctors believe that both outside stressors as well as internal gene manifestations helped for me to cross over the limits or boundaries if you will in my mind. It is my educated guess that the grandiose thoughts, ideas of reference, paranoia, and hallucinations were my mind's way of distracting or escaping itself from all of the strain as a defense mechanism just to survive. I do, however, know there is some damage to my brain, and I will be disabled to some degree the rest of my life by the mere fact that I am living with a degenerative schizoaffective mental illness. I will be on medication the rest of my life, my cross, and my journey.